Daily Oral Grammar

ELEMENTS OF
Literature
THIRD COURSE

TRANSPARENCIES
WORKSHEETS

HOLT, RINEHART AND WINSTON
Harcourt Brace & Company

Austin • New York • Orlando • Atlanta • San Francisco • Boston • Dallas • Toronto • London

STAFF CREDITS

Associate Director: Mescal Evler
Manager of Editorial Operations: Robert R. Hoyt
Managing Editor: Bill Wahlgren
Project Editor: Katie Vignery
Component Editor: Colleen Hobbs
Editorial Staff: *Associate Editors,* Kathryn Rogers, Christopher LeCluyse; *Assistant Managing Editors,* Amanda F. Beard, Marie H. Price; *Copyediting Supervisor,* Michael Neibergall; *Senior Copyeditor,* Mary Malone; *Copyeditors,* Joel Bourgeois, Gabrielle Field, Suzi A. Hunn, Jane Kominek, Millicent Ondras, Theresa Reding, Désirée Reid, Kathleen Scheiner; *Editorial Coordinators,* Robert Littlefield, Mark Holland, Jill O'Neal, Marcus Johnson, Tracy DeMont; *Assistant Editorial Coordinator,* Summer Del Monte; *Support Staff,* Lori De La Garza, Pat Stover, Matthew Villalobos; *Word Processors,* Ruth Hooker, Margaret Sanchez, Kelly Keeley, Elizabeth Butler
Permissions: Tamara A. Blanken, Ann B. Farrar
Design: *Art Director, Book Design,* Richard Metzger; *Design Manager, Book & Media Design,* Joe Melomo
Prepress Production: Beth Prevelige, Simira Davis, Sergio Durante, Belinda Barbosa
Media Production: *Production Manager,* Kim A. Scott; *Production Coordinator,* Belinda Barbosa; *Production Supervisor,* Nancy Hargis
Manufacturing Coordinators: Michael Roche, Belinda Barbosa

Printed in the United States of America

ISBN 0-03-053104-7

3 4 5 6 7   27   02 01 00

CONTENTS

ABOUT THE DAILY ORAL GRAMMAR EXERCISES

One of the most effective ways to teach grammar and language skills is through literature. As students read literature, teachers can help students make connections between an author's use of language and the students' writing. The result is an instructional experience in which literature and language skills are not fragmented.

The purpose of the Daily Oral Grammar transparencies and worksheets is to teach and review sentence construction, usage, and mechanics skills in the context of great literature. Each Daily Oral Grammar exercise is focused on a specific *Elements of Literature* reading selection. The exercises may include information on content, background, author biography, or literary elements. Exercises are keyed to students' reading assignments and can introduce selection materials or themes.

Each exercise is structured according to a standardized testing format used to assess grammar and language skills. This structure allows students an opportunity to practice these skills in the classroom while becoming familiar with a standardized testing format. The exercises consist of three types of multiple-choice questions for testing sentence construction, usage, and mechanics. The chart below describes the three types of Daily Oral Grammar exercises and how they relate to skills generally tested on standardized tests.

Each Daily Oral Grammar transparency includes an answer key that does not appear on the screen when the transparency is projected. The identical exercise, without the answer key, is provided in the form of a blackline master that may be copied and distributed.

DAILY ORAL GRAMMAR INSTRUCTION	SKILL
Students practice sentence construction by reviewing several revision options and determining which version makes the sentence most clear and concise.	Recognizing appropriate sentence construction within the context of a written passage
Students review appropriate usage by choosing the correct word or group of words needed to complete a sentence. Students look at sentence context and then determine the appropriate verb tense or number, the correct pronoun, or the correct form of adjective or adverb.	Recognizing appropriate English usage within the context of a written passage
Students review spelling, capitalization, and punctuation by reading an underlined section in the sample paragraph and identifying the type of error. In each underlined section, either an error has been included or students are asked to select the "no error" option.	Recognizing appropriate spelling, capitalization, and punctuation within the context of a written passage

The following correlation chart lists the skills practiced in each Daily Oral Grammar exercise. The chart shows skills taught on each transparency, as well as references to the relevant instruction in the Language Handbook of the Pupil's Edition.

DAILY ORAL GRAMMAR TRANSPARENCY CORRELATIONS

DAILY ORAL GRAMMAR TRANSPARENCY	ITEM NUMBER	SKILLS TESTED	LANGUAGE HANDBOOK RULES (PUPIL'S EDITION pp. 993–1039)
1 **The Most Dangerous Game**	1	Subject-verb agreement; verb tense	2a, 3a, 3d(1), 3e
	2	Object pronouns	4d
	3	Subject-verb agreement; verb tense	2a, 3a, 3d(1), 3e
	4	Possessive pronouns	charts, pp. 1001, 1029; 14c
2 **A Sound of Thunder**	1	End punctuation	12b
	2	Commas: dependent clauses	12i
	3	Spelling	15d
	4	Spelling	15d
3 **The Birds**	1	Subject pronouns	4a
	2	Possessive pronouns	charts, pp. 1001, 1029; 14c
	3	Verb tense	3a, 3d(1)
	4	Adjective usage	charts, pp. 993, 1003
4 **Poison**	1	Commas in letters	12l(2)
	2	Commas: introductory words	12j(1)
	3	Commas: direct address	12k(2)
	4	Capitalization in letters	11b
5 **The Interlopers**	1	Verb tense	3a, 3d(4)
	2	Adjective usage	charts, pp. 993, 1003
	3	Possessive pronouns	charts, pp. 1001, 1029; 14c
	4	Double negatives	p. 1036
6 **Thank You, M'am**	1	Quotation marks	13c
	2	Commas: introductory phrases	12j(3)
	3	End punctuation	12b
	4	Commas in letters	12l(2)
7 **Harrison Bergeron**	1	Commas in a series	12f
	2	Apostrophes: contractions (no error)	14g
	3	Colons	12q(1)
	4	Spelling	15f
8 **A Christmas Memory**	1	Spelling	15l(2)
	2	Apostrophes: contractions	14g
	3	Spelling	15b (exceptions)
	4	Capitalization: proper nouns	11d(2)
9 **A Man Called Horse**	1	Adjective usage	charts, pp. 993, 1003
	2	Verb tense	3a, 3c, 3d(1)
	3	Adjective usage	5a(2), 5b
	4	Verb tense	3a, 3d(1), 3e
10 **Salvador Late or Early**	1	Capitalization in letters	11b
	2	Spelling	15f
	3	Commas: conjunctions	12h
	4	Commas: dates	12l(1)
11 **The Gift of the Magi**	1	Subject-verb agreement; verb tense	2a, 3d(1)
	2	Subject-verb agreement	2a
	3	Subject-verb agreement; verb tense	2a, 2b, 3d(1)
	4	Object pronouns	4e
12 **Snow**	1	Run-on sentences	9b
	2	Combining sentences	10c

DAILY ORAL GRAMMAR TRANSPARENCY	ITEM NUMBER	SKILLS TESTED	LANGUAGE HANDBOOK RULES (PUPIL'S EDITION pp. 993–1039)
13 **The Necklace**	1 2 3 4	Comparative and superlative adjectives Object of a preposition Subject pronouns Verb tense	5a(1), 5b 6b 4a 3d(1)
14 **The Cask of Amontillado**	1 2 3 4	Capitalization: proper nouns Spelling Commas: dependent clauses End punctuation (no error)	11d(6) 15l(2) 12j(4) 12a
15 **The Gift**	1 2	Run-on sentences Combining sentences (no error)	9b 10a–10e
16 **Blues Ain't No Mockin Bird**	1 2	Sentence fragments Run-on sentences	9a 9b
17 **Marigolds**	1 2	Run-on sentences Sentence fragments	9b 9a
18 **American History**	1 2 3 4	Adverb usage Subject-verb agreement; verb tense Subject-verb agreement; verb tense Comparative and superlative adjectives	charts, pp. 993, 1003 2a, 3d(1) 3a, 3d(1), 3e 5a(5), 5b
19 **Helen on Eighty-sixth Street**	1 2 3 4	Capitalization: proper nouns Commas: appositive phrases Apostrophes: possessives Spelling	11d(2) 12k(1) 14a 15h
20 **The Scarlet Ibis**	1 2 3 4	Commas: introductory phrases Apostrophes: contractions Spelling Commas between adjectives	12j(2) 14g 15g 12g
21 **Not Much of Me**	1 2 3 4	Subject-verb agreement; verb tense Verb tense Subject-verb agreement; verb tense Possessive pronouns	2a, 3a, 3c, 3d(4) 3a, 3c, 3d(4) 2a, 3a, 3d(1) charts, pp. 1001, 1029; 14c
22 **"When I Lay My Burden Down"**	1 2 3 4	Apostrophes: contractions Commas between city and state Commas (no error) Commas: appositives	14g 12l(1) 12i 12k(1)
23 **Choice: A Tribute to Dr. Martin Luther King, Jr.**	1 2 3 4	Punctuation: abbreviations Apostrophes: possessives Capitalization: proper nouns Commas: prepositional phrases	12e 14a 11d(2) 12j(3)
24 **The Talk**	1 2 3 4	Commas: prepositional phrases Capitalization: direct quotes End punctuation End punctuation (no error)	12j(3) 13d 12b 12b
25 **The Best Gift of My Life**	1 2 3 4	Commas: direct quotes Quotation marks Commas (no error) Commas: nonessential phrases	13f(1) 13c 12i 12i
26 **Riding Is an Exercise of the Mind**	1 2	Combining sentences Run-on sentences	10d 9b
27 **"Haven't I Made a Difference!"**	1 2 3 4	Subject-verb agreement; verb tense Verb tense Possessive pronouns Subject pronouns	3a, 3c, 3d(2) 3a, 3c, 3d(2) charts, pp. 1001, 1029 4a

DAILY ORAL GRAMMAR TRANSPARENCY	ITEM NUMBER	SKILLS TESTED	LANGUAGE HANDBOOK RULES (PUPIL'S EDITION pp. 993–1039)
28 The Round Walls of Home	1 2 3 4	Commas (no error) Spelling Apostrophes: contractions Capitalization: proper nouns	12j(3) 15l(4) 14g 11d (5–note)
29 The Loophole of Retreat	1 2 3 4	Double negatives Subject-verb agreement; verb tense Subject-verb agreement; verb tense Adjective usage	p. 1036 2a, 3d(1) 2a, 3d(1) charts, pp. 993, 1003
30 from An Indian's Views of Indian Affairs	1 2 3 4	Commas: introductory clauses Capitalization: proper nouns Apostrophes: possessives Capitalization (no error)	12j(4) 11d(6) 14b 11d(1)
31 Darkness at Noon	1 2 3 4	Possessive pronouns Adverb usage Subject-verb agreement; verb tense Possessive pronouns	charts, pp. 1001, 1029; 14c charts, pp. 993, 1003 2a, 3d(3) charts, pp. 1001, 1029; 14c
32 Homeless	1 2	Combining sentences Combining sentences	10c 10b
33 Misspelling	1 2 3 4	Apostrophes: contractions Commas: conjunctions Spelling Commas: conjunctions	14g 12h 15d 12h
34 Fog	1 2 3 4	Capitalization: quotes Apostrophes: possessives Capitalization (no error) Capitalization: titles	11a(1) 14a 11d(1) 11f(3)
35 in Just–	1 2 3 4	Apostrophes: contractions Capitalization: proper adjectives Commas: nonessential phrases (no error) Commas: appositives	14g 11d(6) 12i 6g
36 I Never Saw a Moor	1 2 3 4	Subject-verb agreement; verb tense Subject-verb agreement; gerunds Subject-verb agreement; verb tense Possessive pronouns	2a, 2c, 3a, 3d(1) 6d 3a, 3d(1), 3e charts, pp. 1001, 1029
37 The Secret	1 2 3 4	Subject pronouns Comparative and superlative adjectives Adverb usage Subject-verb agreement; verb tense	4a 5a(1), 5b charts, pp. 993, 1003 2a, 3d(1)
38 Women	1 2 3 4	Object pronouns Subject-verb agreement; verb tense Adjective usage Comparative and superlative adjectives	4e 2a, 3d(1) charts, pp. 993, 1003 5a(5), 5b
39 Fifteen	1 2 3 4	End punctuation End punctuation End punctuation Commas: conjunctions	12a 12b 12b 12h
40 Legal Alien/ Extranjera legal	1 2 3 4	Commas: introductory clauses Apostrophes: possessives Spelling End punctuation	12j(4) 14a p. 1038 12a
41 The Road Not Taken	1 2 3 4	Capitalization: titles Commas: dependent clauses Colons between hours and minutes End punctuation	11f(1) 12i 12r(1) 12d

DAILY ORAL GRAMMAR TRANSPARENCY	ITEM NUMBER	SKILLS TESTED	LANGUAGE HANDBOOK RULES (PUPIL'S EDITION pp. 993–1039)
42 *The Miracle Worker,* **Part One**	1 2	Run-on sentences Sentence fragments	9b 9a
43 *The Miracle Worker,* **Part Two**	1 2 3 4	Subject-verb agreement; verb tense Adverb usage Object pronouns Double negatives	2a, 3d(1) charts, pp. 993, 1003 4d p. 1036
44 *The Tragedy of Romeo and Juliet,* **Part One**	1 2 3 4	Commas: appositives Capitalization: titles Quotation marks End punctuation	6g 11f(1) 13c 12a, 12c
45 *The Tragedy of Romeo and Juliet,* **Part Two**	1 2 3 4	Subject-verb agreement; verb tense Apostrophes: contractions Possessive pronouns Subject-verb agreement	2a, 3a, 3c, 3d(2) 14g charts, pp. 1001, 1029; 14c 2a
46 *The Odyssey,* **Part One, 1**	1 2 3 4	Adverb usage Pronoun *who* Adjective usage Possessive pronouns	5a(5) 4f charts, pp. 993, 1003 charts, pp. 1001, 1029; 14c
47 *The Odyssey,* **Part One, 2**	1 2 3 4	Possessive pronouns Subject-verb agreement; verb tense Subject-verb agreement; verb tense Participial phrases	charts, pp. 1001, 1029; 14c 2a, 3a, 3c, 3d(4) 2a, 3a, 3c, 3d(2) 6c(2)
48 *The Odyssey,* **Part Two, 1**	1 2 3 4	Colons before a list End punctuation (no error) Commas: conjunctions (no error) Apostrophes: contractions	12q(1) 12a 12h 14g
49 *The Odyssey,* **Part Two, 2**	1 2	Run-on sentences Combining sentences	9b 10b

OPTIONS FOR USING THE DAILY ORAL GRAMMAR EXERCISES

You may tailor the use of Daily Oral Grammar exercises to the needs of the classroom, using them for both instruction and assessment.

- **Linking Literature and Grammar**
  Exercises are based on selections from the Pupil's Edition, providing a useful introduction to selection materials or themes. Conveying information about literary texts in this format allows you to practice standardized testing within the context of students' reading assignments.

- **Practice for Standardized Tests**
  The Daily Oral Grammar exercises provide students with opportunities for practice with a standardized test format. The exercises offer three question types that help familiarize students with sentence construction, usage, and editing skills.

- **Focused Review**
  The Daily Oral Grammar exercises can be used as quick, five- to ten-minute review activities. This use of the exercises is most effective when students discuss and explain their corrections orally. Encouraging students to interpret and explain their answers may lead to useful discussions about grammar, usage, and sentence-writing skills.

- **Building English Language Proficiency**
  The Daily Oral Grammar exercises also can help English-language learners process information about sentence construction, grammar, usage, and mechanics. The exercises help special-needs students break down language information into its basic parts. The frequent, short review of these language basics lets special-needs students build on manageable concepts without becoming overwhelmed by unfamiliar rules.

- **Targeting Strengths and Weaknesses**
  Teachers may choose to use these exercises as a diagnostic tool to help identify students who require further instruction in particular concepts. Blackline masters and transparencies allow teachers to assess students individually or in a classroom group.

ABOUT THE SAMPLE LESSONS

The following pages contain sample lessons for selected Daily Oral Grammar exercises. Each lesson reflects a teacher option for using the transparency. The lessons also illustrate how the Daily Oral Grammar exercises can be used to align instruction and assessment for maximum student learning.

SAMPLE LESSON A: Linking Literature and Grammar

RIDING IS AN EXERCISE OF THE MIND, PUPIL'S EDITION PAGE 401

INSTRUCTIONAL PLAN

- Using Transparency 26, have each student select the correct answer to each of the two exercise items and write a brief explanation of why each answer was chosen.
- Have students get into pairs to discuss their choices and explanations.
- As a class, discuss the responses and explanations for correcting the passage. Discussion questions might include the following:

    Which pairs of you disagreed about your answers?

    What were your disagreements?

    How did you work through your disagreements?

    Which pairs of you agreed about your answers?

    Upon what rules of sentence structure did you base your choices?

    What strategies did you use to determine the correct answers?

- Discuss with students how this lesson focuses on writing complete sentences and writing effective sentences. First, have students turn to the section on writing complete sentences in the Language Handbook (Pupil's Edition, page 1014). Clarify that the second sentence in Transparency 26 is a fragment because there is no subject, thereby eliminating choice D as the correct choice.
- Discuss the two strategies noted on page 1014 that a writer can use to correct sentence fragments. Have students observe that choices A, B, and C all attempt to use strategy 2—attaching the fragment to the sentence that comes before or after it. However, only one of those choices represents the best way to attach the fragment. Note that many times, as in this example, some words may need to be changed or omitted when using this strategy.
- Next, read and discuss with students the definition and the two kinds of run-on sentences highlighted in the Language Handbook (Pupil's Edition, pages 1014–1015). Help students analyze the answer choices for question 2 on Transparency 26: First, have them identify the original sentence as an example of a comma splice; therefore, answer choice J

cannot be the answer. Next, have students determine that answer choice H is an example of a fused sentence, which cannot be the correct answer.

- Before discussing answer choices A and B, read and discuss with students the five strategies for correcting a run-on sentence that are discussed in the Language Handbook (Pupil's Edition, pages 1014–1015). Have students pair up to identify which strategy was used for answer choice A (use a semicolon) and which strategy was used for answer choice B (change one of the complete thoughts into a subordinate clause). As a class, have students discuss how one answer can be incorrect even if both strategies are properly used.
- In the "Quickwrite" section (Pupil's Edition, page 400), students are asked to write in preparation for the reading of "Riding Is an Exercise of the Mind." Have students complete the writing according to the instructions. After students have read the story, have them work in pairs to complete the "Reading Check" exercise (Pupil's Edition, page 404). Have each pair of students write two sentences illustrating two of the revision rules for run-on sentences discussed in the Language Handbook (Pupil's Edition, pages 1014–1015). Have each pair share their sentences with the whole class. The teacher can use this as a check to ensure student proficiency in writing these types of sentences as well as a review of the major events of the story.

ASSESSMENT

1. Collect all of the sentences shared as samples from the student activity above. Select a few to rewrite them incorrectly. Prepare a written or multiple-choice assessment similar to Transparency 26 requiring students to write or identify the correct sentence.

2. Have students revise their initial Quickwrite to model the author's descriptive use of sensory details. Each student's writing will be assessed on the use of sensory details and the ability to write complete and effective sentences.

SAMPLE LESSON B: Practice for Standardized Tests

THE GIFT OF THE MAGI, PUPIL'S EDITION PAGE 202

INSTRUCTIONAL PLAN

- Using Transparency 11, have each student select the correct answer to each of the four exercise items and write a brief explanation of why each answer was chosen.
- Have students work in pairs to discuss their choices and explanations.
- As a class, discuss the responses and explanations for correcting the passage. Discussion questions might include the following:

  Which pairs of you disagreed about your answers?

  What were your disagreements?

  How did you work through your disagreements?

  Which pairs of you agreed about your answers?

  Upon what rules of grammar usage did you agree?

- If students are having trouble with consistency of verb tense (questions 1, 2, and 3), first review the six tenses in the Language Handbook (Pupil's Edition, pages 999–1000). Discuss rule 3(e), stressing the importance of maintaining consistency in verb tense. In addition, discuss the Tips for Writers section. Have students work in pairs or small groups on the "Try It Out" exercise for "Using Appropriate Verb Tenses." Provide students with the correct responses and have the pairs or small groups check their work. Discuss any questions or problems.
- If students are having trouble with pronoun case (#4), have them turn to the "Using Pronouns" section in the Language Handbook (Pupil's Edition, page 1001). Review the definition of *case* and the three different ways pronouns are used in sentences. Emphasize that rule 4(e) (Pupil's Edition, page 1002) is the rule applied in question 4 on Transparency 11.
- Discuss with students how many standardized tests will use the testing format that they have been working with to assess a student's ability to use the English language properly. As a class, discuss strategies that can be used with this type of testing format. Discussion questions might include the following:

What strategies did you use during the exercise?

What strategies are useful in getting to the right answer with this type of test?

How did writing your explanation help you reach the correct answer?

- Provide students with an overhead transparency of the following paragraph:

  O. Henry, whose real name was William Sydney Porter, wrote "The Gift of the Magi." Written in the language of common people, O. Henry's short stories appealed to a broad range of readers in his day. He often showed his sympathy for the weaknesses of ordinary people in the more than six hundred stories he wrote in his lifetime. O. Henry's natural portrayal of his characters made his readers feel an immediate connection to their own lives.

Have students work in pairs or small groups to transform the paragraph into a standardized test prompt similar to Transparency 11. Each pair or small group will identify places for four blanks and compose four multiple-choice questions with responses, complete with answer key. The places chosen for blanks should cite the rules for verb tense consistency and pronoun case studied in the Language Handbook (Pupil's Edition, pages 999–1002).

ASSESSMENT

1. Have each student compose three separate original sentences: one illustrating verb tense consistency, one illustrating the use of the nominative pronoun, and one illustrating the use of the objective pronoun.

2. After students have read the short story, have each student compose a retelling of the story following the guidelines presented in "Reading Check," (Pupil's Edition, page 209). Students should demonstrate their proficiency in maintaining consistency in verb tense and their ability to use nominative and objective pronouns correctly.

SAMPLE LESSON C: Focused Review

THE SCARLET IBIS, PUPIL'S EDITION PAGE 315

INSTRUCTIONAL PLAN

- Using Transparency 20, have each student select the correct answer to each of the four exercise items and write a brief explanation of why each answer was chosen.
- Have students work in pairs to discuss their choices and explanations.
- As a class, discuss the responses and explanations for correcting the passage. Discussion questions might include the following:

    Which pairs of you disagreed about your answers?
    What were your disagreements?
    Which pairs of you agreed about your answers?
    Upon what rules of mechanics did you agree?
    What rules of mechanics did you reference as you discussed your answers?

- Have students turn to the section on spelling in the Language Handbook (Pupil's Edition, pages 1031–1032). Review the structural components of words, highlighting the importance of learning the spelling of the more common roots, prefixes, and suffixes. Note the correct spelling of the suffix *-ful* and discuss the common confusion in spelling words that end with this suffix with its meaning (*-full*).
- Note that questions 1, 2, and 4 require students to be knowledgeable about two specific punctuation rules: apostrophes and commas. First, have students turn to the section on punctuation rules for the apostrophe in the Language Handbook (Pupil's Edition, page 1029). Highlight specifically rule 14(g) that relates to question 2 on the exercise. Discuss the difference between contractions and possessive pronouns by examining the chart at the bottom of the page.
- Organize students into groups of seven. Have students turn to the section on commas in the Language Handbook (Pupil's Edition, page 1023). Assign each person in each group to read and study one of the seven comma rules, 12 (f–l), (Pupil's Edition, pages 1023–1025). Tell students that each one of them will be responsible for teaching his group about his assigned rule. Allow five to seven minutes for silent reading and studying; allow each student two minutes to teach his group about his assigned rule. During the 15 minutes allotted for this activity, monitor the students' presentations and be prepared to clarify any confusion with the whole class. Ask each group to identify which of the seven comma rules has been ignored in question 4 on Transparency 11. Then, have each group compose two original sentences that illustrate the two components of rule 12(g) and share the sentences with the whole class.

ASSESSMENT

1. Have each student compose four original sentences incorporating important ideas or events from "The Scarlet Ibis" that demonstrate the following capitalization and punctuation rules:

    the capitalization rules for proper nouns and proper adjectives
    the proper use of the apostrophe in a contraction
    the proper use of a comma to separate two or more adjectives preceding a noun
    Discussion of the "Making Meanings" exercises (Pupil's Edition, page 325) can provide a foundation for this assessment.

2. Have each student compose seven original sentences on any topic, one for each of the seven comma rules discussed in the Language Handbook (Pupil's Edition, pages 1023–1025).

3. After students have read the short story, have them compose a response to "Connecting with the Text" question 7, or "Extending the Text" question 8 (Pupil's Edition, page 325). Within the response, students should exhibit spelling proficiency with a selected root, prefix, and suffix from the lists in the Language Handbook (Pupil's Edition, pages 1031–1032).

The Most Dangerous Game

1

Circle the letter next to the word or group of words that belongs in each space.

A character's physical and mental struggles are *conflicts.* If a person is struggling against something outside himself or herself, the conflict is external. If the person __1__ to control some inner problem—such as fear, anger, or homesickness— the conflict is internal. Action stories usually hook __2__ with violent external conflicts. Whatever kind of conflict a story __3__ on, it must be strong. The conflict must keep us glued to __4__ seats.

1 A struggle
   B is struggling
   C was struggling
   D had struggled

2 F us
   G we
   H they
   J it

3 A is builded
   B is build
   C was builded
   D is built

4 F ours
   G ourself
   H our
   J our's

A Sound of Thunder

Identify the type of error, if any, in each underlined passage, and circle the letter next to the correct answer.

Think of a time you have swatted a fly or picked a flower. <u>Do these actions have any long-term</u> <u>consequences.</u> [1] If you <u>could see into the future you</u> <u>might be surprised by</u> [2] the answer. <u>The character</u> <u>in this story gets the opportunity to see unnex-</u> <u>pected</u> [3] outcomes when he travels back in time. <u>He</u> <u>finds that a single butterfly has enormous consse-</u> <u>quences</u> [4] for the future.

---

1 A Spelling
   B Capitalization
   C Punctuation
   D No error

2 F Spelling
   G Capitalization
   H Punctuation
   J No error

3 A Spelling
   B Capitalization
   C Punctuation
   D No error

4 F Spelling
   G Capitalization
   H Punctuation
   J No error

Elements of Literature

Circle the letter next to the word or group of words that belongs in each space.

　　__1__ human beings have an uneasy relationship with nature. Nature has two faces. We see it as a source of beauty and peace, but we fear __2__ sudden, random violence. Extreme weather, volcanoes, earthquakes, even the attacks of tiny creatures such as bacteria, killer bees, and viruses __3__ our life on earth. Perhaps this is why, since ancient times, stories have been told about people who find themselves facing the __4__ side of nature.

---

1 A Us
　B We
　C Them
　D They

2 F it's
　G its'
　H its
　J it

3 A threatens
　B can threaten
　C threatened
　D had threatened

4 F danger
　G dangerously
　H most danger
　J dangerous

Identify the type of error, if any, in each underlined passage, and circle the letter next to the correct answer.

<u>Dear Melanie</u>
1

    I just read the scariest story for homework! It's "Poison," by Roald Dahl. Remember when we thought bugs were crawling <u>on us during our</u>
2
<u>camping trip? Well this</u> story reminds me of that night. If you want to be really <u>scared Melanie,</u>
3
<u>be sure to read this story.</u>

<u>your friend,</u>
4
Vontrece

---

1 A Spelling
  B Capitalization
  C Punctuation
  D No error

3 A Spelling
  B Capitalization
  C Punctuation
  D No error

2 F Spelling
  G Capitalization
  H Punctuation
  J No error

4 F Spelling
  G Capitalization
  H Punctuation
  J No error

Circle the letter next to the word or group of words that belongs in each space.

> Maybe you __1__ of the Hatfields and McCoys, two families that carried on a bitter and __2__ feud for years. "The Interlopers" portrays a similar situation, between two men who wish for nothing more than a chance to kill each other. A sudden predicament transforms __3__ mutual hatred. An ironic twist of fate, however, does not give them __4__ time to benefit from their truce.

1 A hearing
   B have heared
   C heared
   D have heard

2 F dead
   G deadly
   H death
   J deathlike

3 A there
   B they're
   C their
   D their's

4 F any
   G no
   H hardly no
   J barely no

Thank You, M'am   **6**

Identify the type of error, if any, in each underlined passage, and circle the letter next to the correct answer.

Dear Grandma,

<u>Have you heard the saying When the going gets</u>
<u>1</u>
tough, the tough get going?" <u>In very tough times</u>
                                                    2
<u>under harsh conditions</u> people like you get moti-

vated. <u>What makes these folks so strong in spirit.</u>
                          3
<u>Why</u> do people like you turn out to be good? Why

do others go so completely wrong?

<u>Love</u>
4
Your grandson

---

1 A Spelling
   B Capitalization
   C Punctuation
   D No error

2 F Spelling
   G Capitalization
   H Punctuation
   J No error

3 A Spelling
   B Capitalization
   C Punctuation
   D No error

4 F Spelling
   G Capitalization
   H Punctuation
   J No error

Identify the type of error, if any, in each underlined passage, and circle the letter next to the correct answer.

You read and hear satire constantly. Satire is <u>used on talk shows on television comedies in the</u> <u>**1**</u> <u>comics and in the movies.</u> In fact, satire <u>is perva-</u> <u>**2**</u> <u>sive; it's not hard to find</u> a story or movie or televi-sion show that uses it. <u>The methods of satire</u> <u>**3**</u> <u>include: mockery and exaggeration.</u> When <u>some-</u> <u>**4**</u> <u>thing is presented to us as ridiculeous,</u> we have to laugh.

---

1 A Spelling
   B Capitalization
   C Punctuation
   D No error

2 F Spelling
   G Capitalization
   H Punctuation
   J No error

3 A Spelling
   B Capitalization
   C Punctuation
   D No error

4 F Spelling
   G Capitalization
   H Punctuation
   J No error

Identify the type of error, if any, in each underlined passage, and circle the letter next to the correct answer.

<u>dear Salvador,</u>
1

    I know that next week is your birthday. I have

watched you <u>careing for your two little brothers,</u>
                  2

and I know you work hard. You <u>have much respon-</u>
                                3

<u>sibility and you</u> handle it well. I am very proud

of you; I won't forget that <u>October 25 2000,</u> will be
                                4

a special day for you.

Your teacher,

Mrs. Rodriguez

---

1 A Spelling
  B Capitalization
  C Punctuation
  D No error

2 F Spelling
  G Capitalization
  H Punctuation
  J No error

3 A Spelling
  B Capitalization
  C Punctuation
  D No error

4 F Spelling
  G Capitalization
  H Punctuation
  J No error

A Christmas Memory

Identify the type of error, if any, in each underlined passage, and circle the letter next to the correct answer.

> <u>One of the best qualitys of the human spirit is</u>
> <u>1</u>
> <u>generosity</u>—especially the <u>generosity of those who</u>
> <u>2</u>
> <u>dont have much themselves.</u> "A Christmas Memory"
> is about two characters and their Christmas rituals.
> The story reveals something about <u>freindship; it</u>
> <u>3</u>
> <u>also reveals how love endures.</u> Capote's story
> draws on <u>his boyhood in alabama,</u> where he was
> <u>4</u>
> raised by relatives.

1 A Spelling
   B Capitalization
   C Punctuation
   D No error

3 A Spelling
   B Capitalization
   C Punctuation
   D No error

2 F Spelling
   G Capitalization
   H Punctuation
   J No error

4 F Spelling
   G Capitalization
   H Punctuation
   J No error

A Man Called Horse

Circle the letter next to the word or group of words that belongs in each space.

"A Man Called Horse" is a story of the __1__ spirit, of what it can endure and of what it values above all else in life. The story is about a white man who is __2__ captive by the Crow. There is no romanticizing of settlers or of American Indians; rather, there is something more perceptive and __3__. "A Man Called Horse" __4__ in 1845. At that time, the Crow moved frequently over the northern plains.

---

1 A humanly
  B humanely
  C humanity
  D human

2 F take
  G taken
  H took
  J taked

3 A grip
  B grippinger
  C grippingest
  D more gripping

4 F begins
  G begin
  H begun
  J had begun

The Gift of the Magi

Circle the letter next to the word or group of words that belongs in each space.

Often when we read a story, we think one thing will happen, only to be taken by surprise when something entirely different __1__ place. This ironic situation reminds us that even though we think we can control our lives, chance or the unexpected often __2__ the last word. Fiction, like life, __3__ surprises. In "The Gift of the Magi," two characters search for the perfect Christmas gift. What happens to __4__ is not what they expect.

---

1 A take
  B takes
  C taken
  D taking

2 F has
  G have
  H be
  J are

3 A bring
  B brings
  C brought
  D had brought

4 F their
  G themselves
  H them
  J they

Circle the letter next to the best way to revise or combine each underlined section. If the section needs no change, mark "Correct as is."

A new climate can bring surprises, such as sleet,
¹
extreme heat, or it can bring ice. "Snow" is about Yolanda, who moves to New York City. **She has**
²
surprises as she learns about a new city and a new culture. She also has surprises while learning about a new climate.

---

1 A A new climate can bring surprises such as sleet, extreme heat, ice.

   B A new climate can bring surprises such as sleet and extreme heat, ice.

   C A new climate can bring surprises such as sleet, extreme heat, or ice.

   D Correct as is

2 F She has surprises as she learns about a new city, a new culture, new climate.

   G She has surprises as she learns about a new city while also learning about a new culture, climate.

   H She has surprises as she learns about not only a new city and culture, but also about a new climate.

   J Correct as is

The Necklace

Circle the letter next to the word or group of words that belongs in each space.

All of us, at one time or another, have felt that the grass is greener on the other side of the fence—in other words, that someone else's life is __1__ than our own. For some of us, it is wealth and the possessions of __2__ that we envy. __3__ believe that having what they have will make us happy, until we __4__ the unexpected results of envy.

1 A more good
   B gooder
   C more better
   D better

2 F other's
   G others'
   H others
   J otherses

3 A We
   B Us
   C He
   D Them

4 F experienced
   G experience
   H had experienced
   J has experienced

Identify the type of error, if any, in each underlined passage, and circle the letter next to the correct answer.

> Centuries ago, <u>christians buried their dead in</u>
> ₁
> catacombs, which are winding tunnels. Later,
> <u>wealthy familys built</u> catacombs beneath their
> ₂
> homes. <u>Because these chambers were dark and cool</u>
> ₃
> <u>they</u> were suitable not only for burial but also for
> storing wine. Fortunato in Poe's story stumbles into
> a <u>catacomb that is used for both.</u>
> ₄

1 A Spelling
   B Capitalization
   C Punctuation
   D No error

2 F Spelling
   G Capitalization
   H Punctuation
   J No error

3 A Spelling
   B Capitalization
   C Punctuation
   D No error

4 F Spelling
   G Capitalization
   H Punctuation
   J No error

Circle the letter next to the best way to revise or combine each underlined section. If the section needs no change, mark "Correct as is."

We may not celebrate holidays today as our ancestors did. <u>We shop for different gifts we cook</u> <u>with new recipes.</u>
₁ We still choose gifts for people we love, however. <u>Although the holidays have</u> <u>changed in "The Gift," the meaning of Christmas</u> <u>endures.</u>
₂

---

1 A We shop for different gifts, we cook with new recipes.

   B We shop for different gifts, and we cook with new recipes.

   C We shop for different gifts; cooking with new recipes.

   D Correct as is

2 F Although the holidays have changed in "The Gift." The meaning of Christmas endures.

   G The holidays have changed in "The Gift," the meaning of Christmas endures.

   H Although the holidays have changed in "The Gift"; the meaning of Christmas enduring.

   J Correct as is

Circle the letter next to the best way to revise or combine each underlined section. If the section needs no change, mark "Correct as is."

> <u>**The title of this story from an old blues song**</u>
> <u>1</u>
> <u>**sung by African Americans as a response to**</u>
> <u>**trouble.**</u> **The song says that blues music is not about**
> **self-pity or death.** <u>**Blues songs are fighting songs,**</u>
> <u>2</u>
> <u>**they help people survive.**</u>

1 A The title of this story coming from an old blues song sung by African Americans as a response to trouble.

B The title of this story comes from an old blues song sung by African Americans as a response to trouble.

C The title of this story from an old blues song being sung by African Americans as a response to trouble.

D Correct as is

2 F Blues songs are fighting songs they help people survive.

G Blues songs are fighting. Songs they help people survive.

H Blues songs are fighting songs; they help people survive.

J Correct as is

Circle the letter next to the best way to revise or combine each underlined section. If the section needs no change, mark "Correct as is."

In the 1930s, an economic depression swept the world. <u>Banks closed people lost their entire savings.</u>
<u>1</u>
Businesses failed all over America, and factories were shut down. As the narrator of "Marigolds" says, however, the Depression was nothing new to her family. <u>Black workers being used to hard times.</u>
<u>2</u>

---

1 **A** Banks closed, people lost their entire savings.

B Banks closed, and people lost their entire savings.

C Banks closed; and people lost their entire savings.

D Correct as is

2 **F** Black workers used to hard times.

G Black workers were used to hard times.

H Because Black workers were used to hard times.

J Correct as is

Circle the letter next to the word or group of words that belongs in each space.

It might not be so easy to start a friendship, yet it seems __1__ enough. You would like to be friends with somebody who __2__ interesting—nice, smart, talented—from a distance but who is very different from you. Say that person is much older or younger, or is from another country, or __3__ a different language. What do you think would be the __4__ approach?

---

1 A simpler
   B simple
   C simpleton
   D simplest

2 F appear
   G had appeared
   H appearing
   J appears

3 A speaking
   B speak
   C speaks
   D spoke

4 F more good
   G most good
   H better
   J best

Identify the type of error, if any, in each underlined passage, and circle the letter next to the correct answer.

    <u>Helen of troy is one of the most famous charac-</u>
<u>ters in</u> Greek mythology. <u>Her father is Zeus the</u>
                            2
<u>greatest of the</u> Greek gods. Helen was born after
Zeus, in the form of a swan, attacked Leda. <u>Helens</u>
                                                       3
<u>beauty prompts a great war between the Greeks</u>
<u>and the Trojans.</u> The main <u>character in "Helen on</u>
                                          4
<u>Eighty-sixth Street" wants to play the beautyful</u>
<u>and</u> tragic Helen in a school play.

---

1 A Spelling
   B Capitalization
   C Punctuation
   D No error

2 F Spelling
   G Capitalization
   H Punctuation
   J No error

3 A Spelling
   B Capitalization
   C Punctuation
   D No error

4 F Spelling
   G Capitalization
   H Punctuation
   J No error

Identify the type of error, if any, in each underlined passage, and circle the letter next to the correct answer.

<u>Deeply moved by reading "The Scarlet Ibis" many</u> <u>people</u> say it is a story they will never forget. The
1
story is set in the American South. Its climax takes place in 1918, the year World War I ended <u>in Europe.</u>
2
<u>Youll find references in the story</u> to battles being
fought in parts of the world <u>far from this peaceful</u>
3
<u>Southern setting.</u> The story is about a <u>small tragic</u>
4
<u>struggle</u> that takes place between two brothers.

---

1 A Spelling
   B Capitalization
   C Punctuation
   D No error

2 F Spelling
   G Capitalization
   H Punctuation
   J No error

3 A Spelling
   B Capitalization
   C Punctuation
   D No error

4 F Spelling
   G Capitalization
   H Punctuation
   J No error

Circle the letter next to the word or group of words that belongs in each space.

You probably know a lot about Abraham Lincoln from what biographers and historians have written, from what teachers __1__, and from what __2__ on television. All of this information __3__ from people other than Lincoln. What do you think you might learn about Lincoln from Lincoln himself? Do you like __4__ stories and speeches? How would you describe the tone of his writing?

---

1 A says
   B had said
   C have said
   D said

2 F you had seen
   G you saw
   H you seen
   J you've seen

3 A come
   B comes
   C had come
   D coming

4 F his'
   G he's
   H his
   J hims

Identify the type of error, if any, in each underlined passage, and circle the letter next to the correct answer.

<u>We all remember people weve admired</u>—people
 1
who are wise, funny, or especially kind. In this

story, Maya Angelou reflects <u>on an incident from</u>
                                              2
<u>her childhood in Stamps Arkansas</u>. Angelou <u>recalls</u>
                                                        3
<u>a woman who faced difficult circumstances.</u> This

<u>woman, Mrs. Annie Henderson built</u> a new life for
 4
herself.

---

1 A Spelling
   B Capitalization
   C Punctuation
   D No error

2 F Spelling
   G Capitalization
   H Punctuation
   J No error

3 A Spelling
   B Capitalization
   C Punctuation
   D No error

4 F Spelling
   G Capitalization
   H Punctuation
   J No error

Identify the type of error, if any, in each underlined passage, and circle the letter next to the correct answer.

<u>With eloquence and style, Dr. Martin Luther King,</u>
1
<u>Jr, brought</u> the message of civil <u>rights to the worlds</u>
2
<u>television audience.</u> His voice sounded a call for the

<u>elimination of racism in the United states through</u>
3
nonviolent resistance. <u>To a generation of African</u>
4
<u>Americans he</u> became a symbol of the struggle to

fulfill the century-old promise of emancipation.

---

1 A Spelling
   B Capitalization
   C Punctuation
   D No error

2 F Spelling
   G Capitalization
   H Punctuation
   J No error

3 A Spelling
   B Capitalization
   C Punctuation
   D No error

4 F Spelling
   G Capitalization
   H Punctuation
   J No error

Identify the type of error, if any, in each underlined passage, and circle the letter next to the correct answer.

In the <u>autobiography that you are about to</u>
  1
<u>read a twelve</u>-year-old boy who is disgusted with

his <u>own looks says, "people like people</u> with
  2
nice faces." <u>Is he right.</u> How much <u>emphasis does</u>
              3   **4**
<u>our society place on appearances?</u>

1 A Spelling
  B Capitalization
  C Punctuation
  D No error

2 F Spelling
  G Capitalization
  H Punctuation
  J No error

3 A Spelling
  B Capitalization
  C Punctuation
  D No error

4 F Spelling
  G Capitalization
  H Punctuation
  J No error

Identify the type of error, if any, in each underlined passage, and circle the letter next to the correct answer.

The <u>narrator in "The Best Gift of My Life" says</u>
₁
<u>"I think my</u> idea of heaven when I was <u>a kid was</u>
₂
<u>Christy Sanders home. A</u> quick analysis might lead

you to realize that this essay <u>was written by some-</u>
₃
<u>one who, at</u> least <u>at that time in her life longed to</u>
₄
<u>live somewhere else.</u>

1 A Spelling
   B Capitalization
   C Punctuation
   D No error

3 A Spelling
   B Capitalization
   C Punctuation
   D No error

2 F Spelling
   G Capitalization
   H Punctuation
   J No error

4 F Spelling
   G Capitalization
   H Punctuation
   J No error

Circle the letter next to the best way to revise or combine each underlined section. If the section needs no change, mark "Correct as is."

> <u>**Sensory images add color to description. They**</u>
> **1**
> <u>**add life, helping readers to perceive a scene.**</u>
>
> **Momaday's descriptions depict the Navajo riders and their songs.** <u>**We smell pine and smoke, we see**</u>
> **2**
> <u>**the geese above Jemez Pueblo.**</u>

1 A Sensory images add color to description, and they also add life, helping readers to perceive a scene.

B Sensory images add color to description, helping readers to perceive a scene and adding life.

C Sensory images add color and life to description, helping readers to perceive a scene.

D Correct as is

2 F We smell pine and smoke; we see the geese above Jemez Pueblo.

G We smell pine and smoke because we see the geese above Jemez Pueblo.

H We smell pine and smoke we see the geese above Jemez Pueblo.

J Correct as is

"Haven't I Made a Difference!"   **27**

Circle the letter next to the word or group of words that belongs in each space.

Throughout history, pets have made people feel happy. Probably more than fifty thousand years ago cave dwellers __1__ dogs as pets. Ancient Egyptians tamed baboons and worshiped cats. Before the first Europeans arrived in Mexico, the Aztecs __2__ pet parrots. Why do people make animals part of __3__ homes? Is it because pets seem to care about us, or is it because __4__ allow us to care for them?

---

1 A have
   B had
   C has
   D haved

2 F keep
   G keeped
   H keeping
   J kept

3 A them
   B their
   C his or her
   D our

4 F we
   G them
   H it
   J they

Identify the type of error, if any, in each underlined passage, and circle the letter next to the correct answer.

<u>With our feet planted firmly here on the ground,</u>
1
it's hard to hold on to the thought that <u>our compli-
2
cated lifes take place on a planet</u> spinning in space.

<u>Its all a matter of perspective.</u> Picture yourself
3
cruising to Mars. What might <u>you think and feel as
4
you look back at the planet earth?</u>

---

1 A Spelling
  B Capitalization
  C Punctuation
  D No error

2 F Spelling
  G Capitalization
  H Punctuation
  J No error

3 A Spelling
  B Capitalization
  C Punctuation
  D No error

4 F Spelling
  G Capitalization
  H Punctuation
  J No error

Circle the letter next to the word or group of words that belongs in each space.

Imagine a place so small you __1__ stand up, with little air and no light. You can't see the rats, mice, and bugs __2__ on you, but you can feel them. Then, imagine that this is a place where you must __3__ to be safe. The author of "The Loophole of Retreat" lived in such a __4__ hiding place for seven years.

---

1 A cannot hardly
    B cannot never
    C cannot
    D cannot barely

3 A stayed
    B have stayed
    C stay
    D will stay

2 F crawled
    G crawls
    H have crawled
    J crawling

4 F tinier
    G tiny
    H tiniest
    J more tiny

from An Indian's Views of Indian Affairs

Identify the type of error, if any, in each underlined passage, and circle the letter next to the correct answer.

> <u>When Europeans first arrived about ten</u> million
> ₁
> <u>American indians lived in</u> what is today the United
> ₂
> States. <u>The history of the Europeans relationship</u>
> ₃
> with the original inhabitants is tragic. In his speech
> Chief <u>Joseph pleads with the government for better</u>
> ₄
> <u>treatment</u> for his people.

1 A Spelling
   B Capitalization
   C Punctuation
   D No error

3 A Spelling
   B Capitalization
   C Punctuation
   D No error

2 F Spelling
   G Capitalization
   H Punctuation
   J No error

4 F Spelling
   G Capitalization
   H Punctuation
   J No error

Circle the letter next to the word or group of words that belongs in each space.

In "Darkness at Noon," the narrator tells some humorous stories about how people have reacted to __1__ blindness. Although he claims to have a "saintlike disposition," some reactions __2__ annoy him, and others please him. As you read this essay, you __3__ how the narrator wants to be treated. __4__ anecdotes make a point about people's behavior around those with impaired vision.

---

1 A him
  B he
  C his'
  D his

2 F clear
  G clearly
  H cleared
  J clearing

3 A have discover
  B had discovered
  C will discover
  D discovering

4 F His
  G Him's
  H He's
  J His'

Circle the letter next to the best way to revise or combine each underlined section. If the section needs no change, mark "Correct as is."

In this essay Anna Quindlen states her opinions.
1
She also tells stories and shares her feelings.

As you read, notice what Quindlen is trying to per-
2
suade you to do. As well as how she tries to do so.

---

1 A In this essay Anna Quindlen states her opinions, also tells stories and shares feelings.

   B In this essay Anna Quindlen states her opinions stories and feelings.

   C In this essay Anna Quindlen states her opinions, tells stories, and shares her feelings.

   D Correct as is

2 F As you read, notice what Quindlen is trying to persuade you to do as well as how she tries to do so.

   G As you read, notice what Quindlen is trying to persuade you to do; how she tries to do so.

   H As you read, notice what Quindlen is trying to persuade you to do; as well as, how she tries to do so.

   J Correct as is

Misspelling

Identify the type of error, if any, in each underlined passage, and circle the letter next to the correct answer.

<u>Youve probably heard many times that it's</u>
¹
important <u>to spell words correctly but to do so</u>
²
isn't always easy. <u>See what humorous examples of</u>
³
<u>mispellings Charles Kuralt has discovered</u> "on the
road" in the United States. What do you think of the
signs Kuralt <u>mentions, and his wry comments</u> on
⁴
them?

---

1 A Spelling
   B Capitalization
   C Punctuation
   D No error

3 A Spelling
   B Capitalization
   C Punctuation
   D No error

2 F Spelling
   G Capitalization
   H Punctuation
   J No error

4 F Spelling
   G Capitalization
   H Punctuation
   J No error

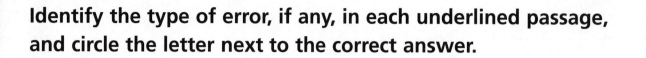

Fog

Identify the type of error, if any, in each underlined passage, and circle the letter next to the correct answer.

> <u>Sandburg never comes right out and says,</u> [1] <u>"the fog is a cat."</u> However, <u>the fogs behavior</u> [2] is certainly like a cat's. <u>Sandburg develops this image</u> [3] throughout the <u>six lines of "fog."</u> [4]

1. A Spelling
   B Capitalization
   C Punctuation
   D No error

2. F Spelling
   G Capitalization
   H Punctuation
   J No error

3. A Spelling
   B Capitalization
   C Punctuation
   D No error

4. F Spelling
   G Capitalization
   H Punctuation
   J No error

Identify the type of error, if any, in each underlined passage, and circle the letter next to the correct answer.

 <u>The strangers lame and goat-footed.</u> If you <u>know
¹   ²
your greek mythology, this</u> description should

sound familiar. Hephaestus, the god of fire, was

lame. <u>Here he is, thousands of years later,</u> to heat
          ³
up this year's spring. Also, <u>Pan the homely god of
                                                          ⁴
nature was goat-footed.</u> Pan, who invented the

flute, is calling children to dance.

---

1 A Spelling
   B Capitalization
   C Punctuation
   D No error

2 F Spelling
   G Capitalization
   H Punctuation
   J No error

3 A Spelling
   B Capitalization
   C Punctuation
   D No error

4 F Spelling
   G Capitalization
   H Punctuation
   J No error

Circle the letter next to the word or group of words that belongs in each space.

> Every day each of us __1__ in our imagination. Yes, that includes thinking about running the marathon or __2__ of being a basketball star. Being a poet means tuning in and paying attention to these journeys—and writing down what they look and __3__ like as they flash by. Emily Dickinson traveled to the ends of the earth in __4__ imagination.

1 A travel
  B traveled
  C travels
  D has traveled

2 F to dream
  G dream
  H dreamed
  J dreaming

3 A feels
  B felt
  C feel
  D feeling

4 F her's
  G she
  H hers
  J her

The Secret   **37**

Circle the letter next to the word or group of words that belongs in each space.

If you knew the secret of life, __1__ would be superhuman. Clearly you're not. However, certain poems can put you in touch with matters __2__ than yourself. Poems can capture bits of life the way plants capture sunlight in their leaves. Once written, these poems wait __3__ for some reader to read them so they can release that stored-up life. Of course, poems __4__ different things to different people.

1 A they
   B we
   C you
   D it

2 F more bigger
   G bigger
   H biggest
   J more big

3 A quiet
   B quieter
   C quietest
   D quietly

4 F reveals
   G revealed
   H has revealed
   J reveal

Circle the letter next to the word or group of words that belongs in each space.

Very few of __1__ are born into this world with large amounts of money. However, every one of us __2__ incalculable treasure. We are the living beneficiaries of everyone who has ever lived. What people before us did with their lives affects ours. If we inherit a polluted planet, they are partially __3__. If they spent their lives struggling to make the world a __4__ place, its improvement is part of their legacy.

---

1 A we
  B us
  C they
  D it

2 F inherits
  G inheriting
  H inherit
  J have inherited

3 A responsibility
  B responsibly
  C responsible
  D response

4 F more good
  G more better
  H better
  J best

Identify the type of error, if any, in each underlined passage, and circle the letter next to the correct answer.

> When you're young, many things seem <u>impossi-</u>
> <u>ble. Think of a moment when</u> you were close to
> something you wanted but couldn't <u>acquire. What</u>
> <u>was it.</u> What feelings did you have after the
> <u>moment passed. Did the incident present</u> you with
> choices? We sometimes come close <u>to things that</u>
> <u>we want,</u> but can't have.

1 A Spelling
  B Capitalization
  C Punctuation
  D No error

2 F Spelling
  G Capitalization
  H Punctuation
  J No error

3 A Spelling
  B Capitalization
  C Punctuation
  D No error

4 F Spelling
  G Capitalization
  H Punctuation
  J No error

Elements of Literature

Legal Alien/Extranjera legal   **40**

Identify the type of error, if any, in each underlined passage, and circle the letter next to the correct answer.

    <u>When you read you</u> can't see the writer's face or
    ₁

gestures. <u>You can't hear the writers voice.</u> Writers
          ₂

have to use words that show you how <u>they feel—</u>
                           ₃

<u>words that express thier tone.</u> Tone may be simple

or complicated—<u>and very changeable</u> Tone is the
                  ₄

attitude a writer takes toward the audience, the sub-

ject, or a character.

---

1 A Spelling
   B Capitalization
   C Punctuation
   D No error

3 A Spelling
   B Capitalization
   C Punctuation
   D No error

2 F Spelling
   G Capitalization
   H Punctuation
   J No error

4 F Spelling
   G Capitalization
   H Punctuation
   J No error

Identify the type of error, if any, in each underlined passage, and circle the letter next to the correct answer.

<u>Dear miss Ward:</u>
1
   I thought of a poem while walking in the <u>forest</u>
                                                    2
<u>which is lovely now.</u> At a crossroads, I met a girl

walking on the other path. Because <u>it was about</u>
                                              3
<u>630 P.M.,</u> I could barely see her, but she resembled

me. I wondered what would happen if I took her

path. Let me know if you are interested in seeing a

<u>poem based on this idea</u>
4
Imaginatively yours,

Roberta Frost

---

1 A Spelling
   B Capitalization
   C Punctuation
   D No error

2 F Spelling
   G Capitalization
   H Punctuation
   J No error

3 A Spelling
   B Capitalization
   C Punctuation
   D No error

4 F Spelling
   G Capitalization
   H Punctuation
   J No error

Circle the letter next to the best way to revise or combine each underlined section. If the section needs no change, mark "Correct as is."

> <u>This play deals with a main character who can-</u>
> ₁
> <u>not speak or hear much of the plot must be shown</u>
>
> <u>physically.</u> Patty Duke originally played the role of
>
> Helen. <u>Later playing the part of Annie in the TV</u>
> ₂
> <u>movie.</u>

1 **A** This play deals with a main character who cannot speak or hear, much of the plot must be shown physically.

B This play deals with a main character who cannot speak or hear, so much of the plot must be shown physically.

C This play deals with a main character. Who cannot speak or hear much of the plot must be shown physically.

D Correct as is

2 **F** Later, she played the part of Annie in the TV movie.

G Later, she being Annie in the TV movie.

H With her later playing the part of Annie in the TV movie.

J Correct as is

Circle the letter next to the word or group of words that belongs in each space.

We __1__ across many doors in a lifetime—doors into relationships, responsibilities, opportunities. If life is easy, the doors open __2__. If life is more difficult, we find that some doors require a lot of effort to open—some stay locked and bolted no matter how we pound at __3__. Often, even with those doors we struggle to open, we __4__ sure what we'll find on the other side.

---

1 A come
   B comes
   C come
   D coming

2 F smooth
   G smoothest
   H smoothly
   J smoother

3 A it
   B them
   C that
   D this

4 F aren't hardly
   G aren't barely
   H aren't never
   J aren't

Identify the type of error, if any, in each underlined passage, and circle the letter next to the correct answer.

    <u>Romeo and Juliet, a very young man and a</u>
1
<u>nearly fourteen-year-old girl fall in</u> love at first sight. They are caught up in an idealized, almost unreal, passionate love, and <u>they convince friar</u>
2
<u>Laurence to marry them.</u> However, instead of living happily ever after, they both die. <u>The play calls</u>
3
<u>Romeo and Juliet a pair of star-crossed</u> lovers."

<u>Alas, how true these words are?</u>
4

---

1 A Spelling
   B Capitalization
   C Punctuation
   D No error

2 F Spelling
   G Capitalization
   H Punctuation
   J No error

3 A Spelling
   B Capitalization
   C Punctuation
   D No error

4 F Spelling
   G Capitalization
   H Punctuation
   J No error

Circle the letter next to the word or group of words that belongs in each space.

Shakespeare __1__ this play about four hundred years ago. __2__ not surprising, then, that many of his words are by now archaic, which means that they (or some of __3__ particular meanings) have disappeared from common use. The side notes in your textbook will help you with these archaic words and with other words and expressions that __4__ unfamiliar to you.

---

1 A write
  B wrote
  C written
  D writed

2 F Its
  G Its'
  H Its's
  J It's

3 A there
  B them
  C they're
  D their

4 F being
  G is
  H are
  J be

Circle the letter next to the word or group of words that belongs in each space.

Once in Troy, Odysseus performed extremely __1__ as a soldier and commander. It was he, for example, __2__ thought of the famous wooden-horse trick, which would lead to the downfall of Troy. For ten years the Greeks had been fighting outside Troy's __3__ walls. They had been unable to break through the walls and enter the city. Odysseus wanted to build a huge, wooden horse and hide a few Greek soldiers inside __4__ hollow belly.

---

1 A good
  B well
  C better
  D best

2 F who
  G whose
  H whom
  J who'se

3 A mass
  B massed
  C massive
  D massively

4 F it's
  G its
  H its'
  J it is

Circle the letter next to the word or group of words that belongs in each space.

> The Greeks pushed the horse up to the gates of Troy and withdrew __1__ armies. Thinking that the Greeks had __2__ up the fight and that the horse was a peace offering, the Trojans __3__ the horse into their city. That night, the Greeks __4__ inside the wooden body came out, opened the gates of Troy to the whole Greek army, and began the battle that was to win the war.

1 A they
  B there
  C their
  D they're

3 A bring
  B bringed
  C brought
  D bringing

2 F give
  G gived
  H gave
  J given

4 F hide
  G hided
  H hides
  J hidden

Identify the type of error, if any, in each underlined passage, and circle the letter next to the correct answer.

We find them in many places movies, TV, the
1
news, books, science labs, art studios, sports teams.

Sometimes we may even find them in our own
2
lives. They're our heroes, and they may be female
3
or male, real or fictional. They set off on the
4
journey that were all taking deep inside: the quest

to discover who we are.

---

1 A Spelling
   B Capitalization
   C Punctuation
   D No error

2 F Spelling
   G Capitalization
   H Punctuation
   J No error

3 A Spelling
   B Capitalization
   C Punctuation
   D No error

4 F Spelling
   G Capitalization
   H Punctuation
   J No error

Circle the letter next to the best way to revise or combine each underlined section. If the section needs no change, mark "Correct as is."

> Heroes meet challenges, setbacks, and dangers
> ¹
> they make mistakes, lose their way, and find
>
> it again. Even if they fail, they do it grandly. The
> ²
> *Odyssey* is a story about a soldier. Named Odysseus,
>
> he tries to return from the Trojan War.

1 A Heroes meet challenges, setbacks, and dangers, they make mistakes, lose their way, and find it again.

B Heroes meet challenges, setbacks, and dangers; they make mistakes, lose their way, and find it again.

C Heroes meet challenges. Setbacks, and dangers they make mistakes, lose their way, and find it again.

D Correct as is

2 F The *Odyssey* is a story about a soldier named Odysseus, trying to return from the Trojan War.

G The *Odyssey* is a story about a soldier, his name Odysseus tries to return from the Trojan War.

H The *Odyssey* is a story about a soldier named Odysseus who tries to return from the Trojan War.

J Correct as is